Team Spirit

THE NEW ENGLAND PATRIOTS

BY

MARK STEWART

Content Consultant
Jason Aikens
Collections Curator
The Professional Football Hall of Fame

NORWOODHOUSE PRESS

CHICAGO, ILLINOIS

Norwood House Press
P.O. Box 316598
Chicago, Illinois 60631

For information regarding Norwood House Press, please visit our website at:
www.norwoodhousepress.com or call 866-565-2900.

PHOTO CREDITS:
All photos courtesy AP/Wide World Photos, Inc. except the following:
Topps, Inc. (7, 9, 20, 21, 28, 34, 36, 37, 40, 43)
Special thanks to Topps, Inc.

Editor: Mike Kennedy
Designer: Ron Jaffe
Project Management: Black Book Partners, LLC.

Special thanks to: Jason Sienicki and Kathleen Baxter.

LIBRARY OF CONGRESS CATALOGING-IN-PUBLICATION DATA

Stewart, Mark, 1960-
    The New England Patriots / by Mark Stewart, Jason Aikens.
        p. cm. -- (Team spirit)
    Summary: "Presents the history, accomplishments and key personalities of
the New England Patriots football team. Includes timelines, quotes, maps,
glossary and websites"--Provided by publisher.
    Includes bibliographical references and index.
    ISBN-13: 978-1-59953-006-2 (library edition : alk. paper)
    ISBN-10: 1-59953-006-6 (library edition : alk. paper) 1. New England
Patriots (Football team)--History--Juvenile literature. I. Aikens, Jason. II.
Title. III. Series.
    GV956.N36S84 2006
    796.332'640974461--dc21
                                                                2005034509

Manufactured in the United States of America in North Mankato, Minnesota
162R-052010

COVER PHOTO: The New England Patriots celebrate a great
defensive play during a 2003 game.

Table of Contents

SPORTS WORDS & VOCABULARY WORDS: In this book, you will find many words that are new to you. You may also see familiar words used in new ways. The glossary on page 46 gives the meanings of football words, as well as "everyday" words that have special football meanings. These words appear in **bold type** throughout the book. The glossary on page 47 gives the meanings of vocabulary words that are not related to football. They appear in ***bold italic type*** throughout the book.

Meet the Patriots

Football is a test of speed, size, and strength. The team with more power usually wins, but not always. The New England Patriots, for example, are not the most powerful team in football, yet their players own many championship rings. How is this possible? The Patriots have found that the secret to playing winning football is playing smart football.

The Patriots do not try to *dominate* their opponents. Instead, they try to match their effort on every play. The longer the game goes, the more they learn about a team's strengths and weaknesses. In the fourth quarter, when games are often won and lost, the Patriots are ready to strike.

This book tells the story of the Patriots. They have had good teams and great players over the years. Their games are almost always close and exciting, and they have enjoyed many winning seasons. Still, it took more than 40 years before they won their first championship. As any fan will tell you, however, it was well worth the wait.

The Patriots take the field for Super Bowl XXXVIII in February of 2004.

Way Back When

There are no guarantees when you own a **professional** sports team. Billy Sullivan and his partners knew this when they started the Boston Patriots in 1960. The team was part of the new **American Football League (AFL)**. No one was sure whether the AFL would be a success. Even if it was, many fans doubted whether pro football would survive in the Boston area.

Sports fans in Boston had supported basketball's Celtics, hockey's Bruins, and baseball's Red Sox for many years. During the

LEFT: Babe Parilli holds the football for Gino Cappelletti as he kicks a field goal during a 1964 game. RIGHT: Jim Nance was one of the AFL's best running backs in the late 1960s.

same time, five football teams had played in Boston and all of them lost money. Not many people came out to watch the Patriots in 1960, when they won only five games. The team improved quickly, however, and Sullivan sold enough tickets to keep the Patriots alive.

The Patriots were led by their quarterback, Babe Parilli, and Gino Cappelletti, who was a kicker and receiver. Boston's defense starred linebacker Nick Buoniconti and defensive linemen Larry Eisenhauer and Houston Antwine. In 1963, the team reached the **AFL Championship** game, but lost to the San Diego Chargers. More than 20 years passed before the Patriots got a chance to play for the championship again. In 1971, they moved to a stadium outside of Boston and renamed themselves the New England Patriots.

The Patriots had good teams and good players during this time. Jim Nance was one of the best running backs in football during the

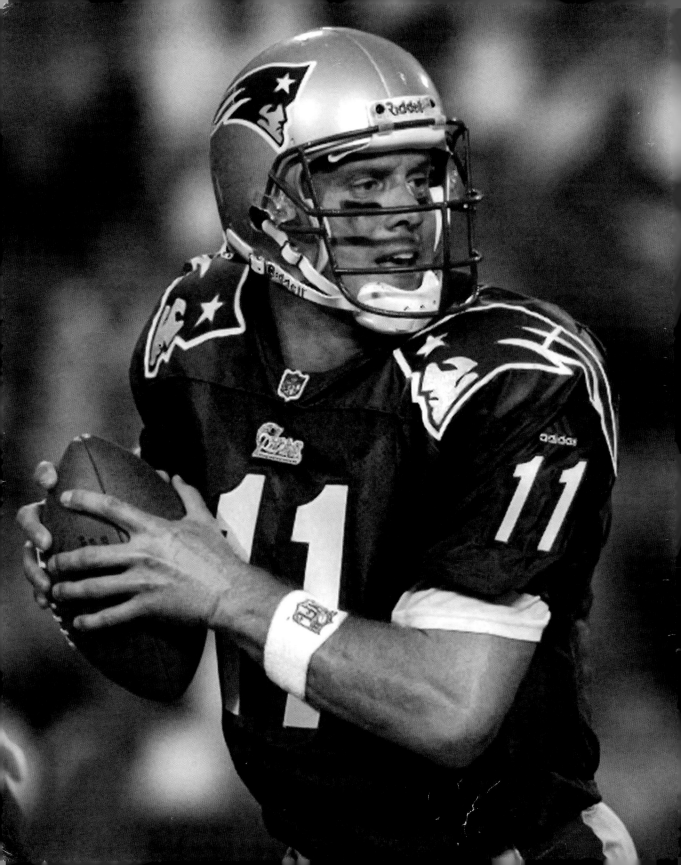

1960s, and Steve Grogan was one of the top quarterbacks from the mid-1970s to the early 1980s. But the Patriots just could not make it to the **Super Bowl**.

In 1984, the Patriots hired Raymond Berry as their head coach. Berry had been a member of the great Baltimore Colts teams of the 1950s and 1960s. In 1985, he led the Patriots to their first **American Football Conference (AFC)** championship. Eleven years later, Bill Parcells coached the team to its second AFC championship. Both times, however, the Patriots lost in the Super Bowl.

Despite their long wait for a Super Bowl victory, New England fans had a lot to be proud of. The team had many excellent players during the 1980s and 1990s, including quarterbacks Tony Eason and Drew Bledsoe, running back Curtis Martin, receiver Terry Glenn, tight end Ben Coates, and defensive stars Andre Tippett, Steve Nelson, Willie McGinest, and Ty Law. All the Patriots needed was a player who could help the team take that final step.

TOP: Tony Eason, the quarterback who helped the Patriots win the AFC Championship in 1985. **LEFT**: Drew Bledsoe drops back to pass. He was the team's starting quarterback for eight seasons.

The Team Today

The Patriots went from being a very good team in the 1990s to playing championship football in recent years. The player who made them great was Tom Brady. Brady did not look like an **All-Pro** quarterback, but he played like one. He was cool under pressure, and his confidence rubbed off on his teammates. In his first season as the team's starting quarterback, he led New England to a thrilling victory in the Super Bowl.

The Patriots win by playing as a team and by not making mistakes. They tackle well and block hard. When one player leaves the team or sits out because of an injury, his replacement is always ready to step in and do a good job.

Because the Patriots do not rely on superstars to win, they always have a chance to go to the Super Bowl. When fans take their seats at the game or tune in on television, they are always very excited. No matter who the team is playing, or who is wearing a New England uniform that day, the Patriots and their supporters feel that no one can stop them if they play their game.

Tom Brady gets ready to call a play.
He gave New England the cool, confident leader the team needed.

Home Turf

The Patriots play their home games at Gillette Stadium. It was built in 2002, and is one of the newest fields in the **National Football League (NFL)**. The stadium is located in Foxborough, Massachusetts, which is south of the city of Boston. The Patriots moved to Foxborough in 1971. Before that, they had a difficult time finding a home. The team played in five different stadiums, including Fenway Park, the home of baseball's Boston Red Sox.

The outside of the Patriots' stadium includes several large *plazas*. This is where fans meet one another before and after games. The stadium was designed to remind fans of New England's *heritage*. The entrance from one of the parking areas has a bridge and lighthouse, structures which are common to the region.

GILLETTE STADIUM BY THE NUMBERS

- *There are 68,756 seats in the stadium.*
- *One luxury "super suite" holds up to 70 fans.*
- *The lighthouse outside the Patriot's field is 12 stories tall.*

The fans in Foxborough watch a kickoff.

Dressed for Success

As you might expect, the Patriots have always worn ***patriotic*** colors. The team's uniform has included red, white, and blue since 1960. Before 1993, the main uniform color was red. The team's helmet showed a ***minuteman*** wearing a tri-corner hat and hiking a football. Since 1993, the team's main uniform color has been blue. The Patriots also began using silver in their jersey, pants, and helmet.

In 1993, the Patriots also designed a new logo. It shows a minuteman wearing a tri-corner hat that is also part of a long, flowing flag. Although some fans liked the old minuteman, most love the new one. They call it "Flying Elvis," because the drawing looks a little bit like the famous singer, Elvis Presley.

Steve Grogan wears the uniform the team used for more than 30 years.

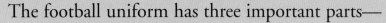

UNIFORM BASICS

The football uniform has three important parts—
- Helmet
- Jersey
- Pants

Helmets used to be made out of leather, and they did not have facemasks—ouch! Today, helmets are made of super-strong plastic. The uniform top, or jersey, is made of thick fabric. It fits snugly around a player so that tacklers cannot grab it and pull him down. The pants come down just over the knees.

There is a lot more to a football uniform than what you see on the outside. Air can be pumped inside the helmet to give it a snug, padded fit. The jersey covers shoulder pads, and sometimes a rib-protector called a "flak jacket." The pants include pads that protect the hips, thighs, *tailbone*, and knees.

Football teams have two sets of uniforms— one dark and one light. This makes it easier to tell two teams apart on the field. Almost all teams wear their dark uniforms at home, and their light ones on the road.

Deion Branch models the team's modern uniform.

We Won!

Ty Law gives Otis Smith a ride as they celebrate New England's victory in Super Bowl XXXVI.

The Patriots have a winning *tradition* that dates back more than four *decades*. Yet it was not until a few years ago that a championship banner finally flew over their stadium. New England's first Super Bowl victory was one of the best sports stories of the year. During the 2001 season, the team lost its starting quarterback, Drew Bledsoe, to a serious injury. His replacement was Tom Brady. Brady had thrown only three passes in the NFL. Many fans believed the team's season was over.

What they did not know was that Brady had been preparing for this day his whole life. He did so well that he remained the starter. The Patriots came together behind their young quarterback, and made it all the way to Super Bowl XXXVI, in February of 2002. The experts

Tom Brady and coach Bill Belichick embrace after Super Bowl XXXVIII.

thought they would lose to the St. Louis Rams, but the Patriots proved they were a special team. They won 20–17 on the last play of the game, when Adam Vinatieri kicked a 48-yard **field goal**.

The Patriots were A.F.C. champions again two years later. Brady was now an experienced *veteran*, and his teammates believed they were *invincible* with him running the show. This time New England faced the Carolina Panthers, in Super Bowl XXXVIII. Both teams had great defenses, so the experts thought it would be a low-scoring game. They were wrong again—the two teams scored a total of 61 points. Once again, Vinatieri kicked the winning field goal, this time with four seconds left. The Patriots won 32–29.

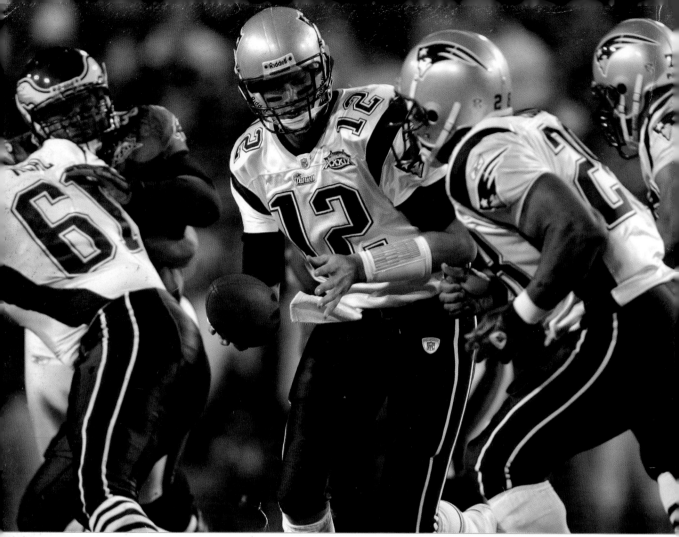

Tom Brady hands off to Corey Dillon in New England's
victory over the Eagles in Super Bowl XXXIX.

One year later, the Patriots were back in the Super Bowl. Their
opponents, the Philadelphia Eagles, kept the game close until the
fourth quarter. New England scored 10 points to go ahead 24–14.
The Eagles tried to come back, but the Patriot's defense made two
big plays, and New England won 24–21.

Bill Belichick raises his arms in victory after the Patriots beat the Eagles in Super Bowl XXXIX.

When the Patriots won Super Bowl XXXIX, they became only the second team to win three Super Bowls in four years. How do they compare to history's other great teams? Some would say that they are not as good, because they did not crush their opponents in the Super Bowl, as others did.

Ask someone who has played in the Super Bowl, however, and he will disagree. There is no greater challenge in football than playing your hardest and your best for 60 minutes, when there is a championship **on the line**. Indeed, when it comes to winning the tough games, the Patriots are as good as any team in NFL history.

Go-To Guys

To be a true star in the NFL, you need more than fast feet and a big body. You have to be a "go-to guy"—someone the coach wants on the field at the end of a big game. Patriots fans have had a lot to cheer about over the years, including these great stars…

THE PIONEERS

GINO CAPPELLETTI
BOSTON PATRIOTS   END

GINO CAPPELLETTI   Kicker/Receiver

• BORN: 3/26/1934   • PLAYED FOR TEAM: 1960 TO 1970

When the Patriots discovered Gino Cappelletti, he was a bartender who played touch football twice a week. He made the team in 1960 as a defensive back, and ended up as Boston's best kicker and receiver. Cappelletti was named **Most Valuable Player (MVP)** in 1964.

BABE PARILLI   Quarterback

• BORN: 5/7/1930   • PLAYED FOR TEAM: 1961 TO 1967

Babe Parilli was already an experienced NFL player when he joined the team in 1961. He led the Patriots to four winning seasons in a row. In 1964, he threw for 3,465 yards and 31 touchdowns—more than anyone else in football that season.

JIM NANCE   Running Back

- BORN: 12/30/1942   • DIED: 6/16/1992   • PLAYED FOR TEAM: 1965 TO 1970

Jim Nance was big enough to be a lineman, and fast enough to be a receiver. The Patriots thought he would be a great running back and they were right. Nance set a league record in his second season with 1,458 yards.

JOHN HANNAH   Guard

- BORN: 4/4/1951   • PLAYED FOR TEAM: 1973 TO 1985

John Hannah was the best guard in the NFL when he played. Nicknamed "Hog," he was equally good at blocking for running backs and protecting the quarterback. Hannah was named Lineman of the Year each season from 1978 to 1981.

STEVE GROGAN   Quarterback

- BORN: 7/24/1953   • PLAYED FOR TEAM: 1975 TO 1990

Steve Grogan was a great runner who happened to be a good quarterback. This combination made him a very dangerous player. In his first five seasons as New England's full-time quarterback, the Patriots won 50 games.

MIKE HAYNES   Defensive Back

- BORN: 7/1/1953   • PLAYED FOR TEAM: 1976 TO 1982

No one guarded pass receivers closer than Mike Haynes. He was big, fast, and very physical. Haynes loved the challenge of covering his man one-on-one, and was one of the best ever at it.

LEFT: Gino Cappelletti   **ABOVE**: John Hannah

MODERN STARS

DREW BLEDSOE   Quarterback

• BORN: 2/14/1972 • PLAYED FOR TEAM: 1993 TO 2001

Drew Bledsoe was one of the most dangerous quarterbacks in NFL history. He could throw touchdown passes from anywhere on the field. The Patriots always had a chance when Bledsoe had the ball in his hands.

WILLIE MCGINEST   Defensive End

• BORN: 12/11/1971 • PLAYED FOR TEAM: 1994–2005

When Willie McGinest rushed the quarterback, it almost always took two people to stop him. He exploded off the line and often ran completely around the man blocking him. McGinest made the New England defense one of the NFL's most feared.

ADAM VINATIERI   Kicker

• BORN: 12/28/1972

• PLAYED FOR TEAM: 1996–2005

No one has connected on more kicks under pressure than Adam Vinatieri. He made the game-winning field goals in Super Bowl XXXVI and Super Bowl XXXVIII. His fourth-quarter field goal in Super Bowl XXXIX was the difference in New England's 24–21 victory.

Adam Vinatieri

Ty Law

TY LAW   Defensive Back

- BORN: 2/10/1974
- PLAYED FOR TEAM: 1995 TO 2004

Ty Law loved to make big plays. Fans came to expect a bone-jarring tackle or spectacular **interception** with the game on the line—like in Super Bowl XXXVI, when he returned an interception for a touchdown.

TEDY BRUSCHI   Linebacker

- BORN: 6/9/1973
- PLAYED FOR TEAM: 1996 TO 2008

The Patriots built a championship defense led by Tedy Bruschi, a great tackler who always seemed to be in the right place at the right time. Fans were shocked when he suffered a *stroke* after the 2004 season, then amazed when he returned to the lineup in 2005.

TOM BRADY   Quarterback

- BORN: 8/3/1977   • FIRST SEASON WITH TEAM: 2000

When Tom Brady joined the Patriots in 2000, most people thought he would never be more than a **back-up quarterback**. When he was given the chance to start, he led the team to three Super Bowls in four seasons.

23

On the Sidelines

When a football team hires a new coach, everyone hopes he will make a difference right away. The Patriots have had great luck with their coaches. In 1984, they changed coaches in the middle of the season and made Raymond Berry the coach. The very next season, Berry led the team to Super Bowl XX.

In 1993, the team hired one of the top coaches in the NFL, Bill Parcells. The Patriots had won only two games the year before. Parcells rebuilt the team and they made it to the **playoffs** in 1994. Two seasons later, the Patriots won the AFC title and played in Super Bowl XXXI.

In 2000, Bill Belichick became the coach of the Patriots. He created a defense that depended on timing and teamwork, and did not need star players at every position. This meant he could move fresh players in and out of the game. Under Belichick, the Patriots became Super Bowl champions by outplaying their opponents at the end of close games.

Team owner Robert Kraft and coach Bill Belichick watch the Patriots practice.

One Great Day

When football fans tuned in to watch Super Bowl XXXVI, they were expecting to see the St. Louis Rams **rout** the Patriots. The Rams had an amazing offense that scored 503 points during the regular season, and 74 more in two playoff games. They were led by superstars Kurt Warner, Isaac Bruce, and Marshall Faulk. Meanwhile, few fans outside New England knew about the best players on the Patriots. In fact, only two—Tom Brady and Lawyer Milloy—were invited to play in the **Pro Bowl** that season.

The Patriots believed they had a chance. The Rams, however, were very confident—maybe too confident. New England's coach, Bill Belichick, told his players to wait for St. Louis to commit a mistake—and then make them pay for it. In the second quarter, Warner threw a weak pass to Bruce, and Ty Law intercepted it. He ran all the way to the end zone for a touchdown. A few minutes later, the Rams **fumbled** and Terrell Buckley recovered the ball for the Patriots. Brady threw a touchdown pass to increase the lead to 14–3.

The Rams could not be stopped forever. In the second half, they scored two touchdowns to tie the score at 17–17 with just 90

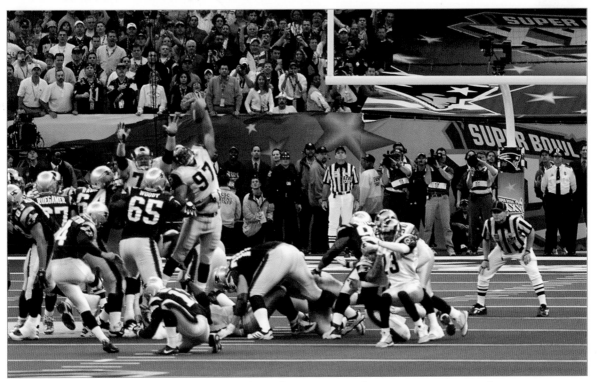

Adam Vinatieri's kick clears the St. Louis line on its way to the
goal posts 48 yards away.

seconds left. That was enough time for Brady and the Patriots, however. He **completed** long passes to Troy Brown and Jermaine Wiggins to put the ball on the 30 yard line with seven seconds left. As time ran out, Adam Vinatieri kicked a field goal to win the game, 20–17.

The Super Bowl victory was the first for the Patriots. It was also the first time a team won football's biggest game on the final play. The Patriots gained only 267 yards in the game, while the Rams piled up 427 yards. But as Bill Belichick had predicted, the team that made the fewest mistakes won the game.

Legend Has It

Was Larry Eisenhauer the Patriots' best all-time tackler?

LEGEND HAS IT that he was. Eisenhauer was a defensive end who was known for bone-rattling hits. His nickname was  the "Wild Man," because he would get very upset when opponents scored on the Patriots. His most famous tackle did not come during a game, but during a children's television show called "Boom Town." The Patriots were supposed to let a tiny clown called Pablo run through all 11 tacklers for a miraculous touchdown. Pablo was almost at the goal line when Eisenhauer chased him down and tackled him very hard. "Nobody gets across our goal line," he yelled, "not even a clown!"

LARRY EISENHAUER def. end

Which Patriots coach gave history's most "shocking" speech?

LEGEND HAS IT that it was Clive Rush. When the team announced that Rush would be the new coach for 1969, he held a *press conference* to meet the local sportswriters. When he grabbed the microphone to start speaking, a surge of electricity went through him and he slumped to the floor. After catching his breath, he joked, "I heard the Boston press was tough, but I never expected this!"

Could Tom Brady have been a professional baseball player?

LEGEND HAS IT that he almost was. Brady was a strong hitter and excellent catcher in high school. The Montreal Expos wanted to sign him in 1995, but he decided to go to college instead. He went to the University of Michigan, where he studied business. Brady was not sure if he would be good enough to play in the NFL, so he made sure to get an education when he had the chance.

It Really Happened

In December of 1982, the Patriots played the Miami Dolphins in a terrible snowstorm. The players were slipping and sliding all day, and neither team could score. The snow was coming down so hard that a snow plow was used to clear off the lines on the field.

With less than five minutes left, the Patriots had the ball on Miami's 16 yard line. New England's coach, Ron Meyer, called a timeout so his kicker, John Smith, could clear off a spot to step before he attempted a field goal. When Meyer saw that Smith could not brush away the ice and snow, he had a brilliant idea. Meyer ordered the man driving the snow plow, Mark Henderson, to clear off a spot that would not be as slippery.

Henderson knew he had to be sneaky about it. He pretended he was clearing off the 20 yard line. When the referees were not looking, he swerved across the spot where Smith would be kicking. Then, before anyone knew what happened, Henderson drove back to the sidelines. Moments later, Smith booted the ball through the **uprights** for the only points either team would score on that cold, miserable day.

Mark Henderson makes the "winning drive" in New England's
3–0 victory over the Dolphins.

The Dolphins demanded that the Patriots be penalized, and that Henderson be punished. The officials could not find a rule against snow plows, and there was nothing they could do to punish Henderson, who did not actually work for the Patriots. New England finished the year with a 5–4 record, which means that Henderson was the difference between a winning season and a losing one!

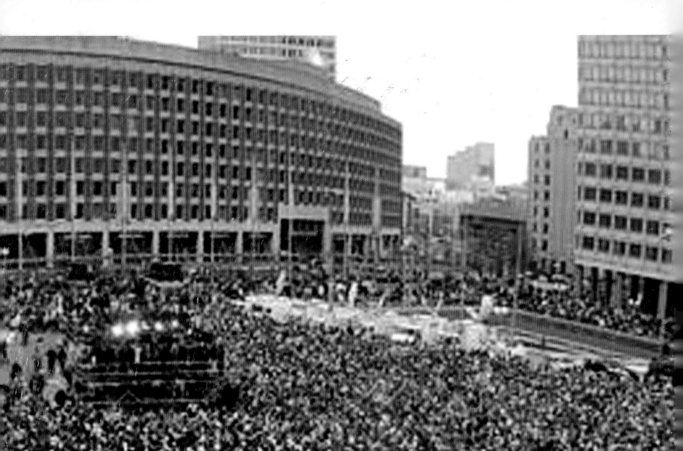

Team Spirit

Because the Patriots represent all of New England, they have "hometown" fans in more states (Connecticut, Massachusetts, Rhode Island, Vermont, New Hampshire, and Maine) than any other team in football. The people of New England believe it is important to be *humble* and respectful—though they can cheer as loudly and proudly as any fans in the NFL. The Patriots have always been a reflection of their fans. Their biggest stars have been quiet, confident players who do not attract much attention.

After winning three Super Bowls in four years, the Patriots have more fans than ever. None, however, are more *dedicated* than the team's famous "mystery man." In 1961, a fan wearing a raincoat ran into the end zone on the last play of a game against the Kansas City Chiefs. He batted away a touchdown pass that would have cost the Patriots the game. The referees could not agree on what to do next, so the Patriots were given the victory.

Fans gather in Boston for the Patriots' victory parade after the team won Super Bowl XXXIX.

Timeline

In this timeline, each Super Bowl is listed under the year it was played. Remember that the Super Bowl is held early in the year, and is actually part of the previous season. For example, Super Bowl XL was played on February 4 of 2006, but it was the championship of the 2005 NFL season.

1964
Babe Parilli leads the league in passing.

1978
Steve Grogan leads the team to the AFC East title.

1960
The Boston Patriots finish their first season with a 5–9 record.

1966
Rookie Jim Nance sets an AFL record with 1,458 rushing yards.

1971
The team moves to Foxborough, Massachusetts and becomes the New England Patriots.

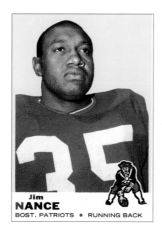

Jim Nance

Steve Grogan

Tony Eason is tackled in Super Bowl XX.

Tom Brady, MVP of Super Bowl XXXVI.

1986
The Patriots win their first AFC championship, but lose to the Chicago Bears in Super Bowl XX.

2002
The Patriots defeat the St. Louis Rams on a last-second field goal to win Super Bowl XXXVI.

1982
The Patriots win the famous "Snow Plow" game.

1997
Drew Bledsoe leads the team to Super Bowl XXXI.

2004
The Patriots beat the Carolina Panthers in Super Bowl XXXVIII.

2005
New England wins Super Bowl XXXIX.

Drew Bledsoe

Fun Facts

Russ Francis

DOUBLY BLESSED

The Patriots have had two of the best tight ends in NFL history. Russ Francis was an All-Pro in the 1970s, and Ben Coates was an All-Pro in the 1990s. The job of the tight end is to block on running plays and catch balls on passing plays.

SMALL WONDER, BIG BAM

One of the best "little men" in NFL history was Mack Herron of the Patriots. He stood a mere 5' 5", but he made a lot of big plays as a running back and **return man**. In 1974, Herron set a record with 2,444 total yards. He shared the **backfield** with Sam "The Bam" Cunningham, who stood 6' 3". In 1977, Cunningham **rushed** for more than 1,000 yards.

SOCCER STYLE

In 1971, New England's kicker was Charlie Gogolak. Gogolak was one of the first soccer-style kickers in the NFL. For almost a century, kickers had used a "straight-ahead" style. Today, all kickers use the soccer style.

OLD SCHOOL

When Tom Brady was named MVP of Super Bowl XXXVI, he was not the first graduate of his high school to win the award. Lynn Swann, who attended Junipero Serra High School during the 1960s, was MVP of Super Bowl X.

OPEN WIDE

Steve Grogan played quarterback for New England longer than anyone, from 1975 to 1990, but he always had a back-up plan. Between seasons, Grogan was a dentist.

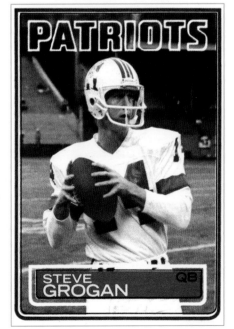

LEFT: Russ Francis
RIGHT: Steve Grogan

Talking Football

"When you work together...great things can be **accomplished**."
—Tedy Bruschi, on teamwork and team spirit

Bill Belichick

"I learn something in this job every day, every week, every year."
—Bill Belichick, on why he loves coaching the Patriots

"You want to be around guys that you share the same goal with...guys who are thirsty and ready to hunt and get victories."
—Corey Dillon, on why he wanted to be traded to the Patriots

"This is really a dream come true. To be the starting quarterback in the Super Bowl is probably the highlight of my life."
—Tom Brady, on reaching his goals as a football player

"Some day I'm going to have kids and tell them that I played on one of the greatest teams of all time."
—*Willie McGinest, on how the Patriots will be remembered*

"The beautiful thing about this team is the way it pulls together when nobody but the team members gives us a chance."
—*Adam Vinatieri, on the thrill of playing for the Patriots*

Willie McGinest

"I run the Patriots like all of my other businesses. I figure out what I can't do and find good people that I can trust."
—*Robert Kraft, on the secret to his success as owner of the Patriots*

For the Record

T he great Patriots teams and players have left their marks on the record books. These are the "best of the best"…

Jim Plunkett

Andre Tippett

PATRIOTS AWARD WINNERS

WINNER	AWARD	YEAR
Gino Cappelletti	AFL Most Valuable Player	1964
Jim Nance	AFL Most Valuable Player	1966
Mike Holovak	AFL Coach of the Year	1966
Jim Plunkett	AFC Rookie of the Year*	1971
Andre Tippett	AFC Defensive Player of the Year	1985
Bill Parcells	NFL Coach of the Year	1994
Curtis Martin	NFL Rookie of the Year	1995
Terry Glenn	AFC Rookie of the Year	1996
Tom Brady	Super Bowl XXXVI MVP	2002
Bill Belichick	NFL Coach of the Year	2003
Tom Brady	Super Bowl XXXVIII MVP	2004
Deion Branch	Super Bowl XXXIX MVP	2005

*An award given to the league's best first-year player.

PATRIOTS ACHIEVEMENTS

ACHIEVEMENT	YEAR
AFL East Champions	1963
AFC East Champions	1978
AFC Champions	1985
AFC East Champions	1986
AFC East Champions	1996
AFC Champions	1996
AFC Champions	2001
Super Bowl XXXVI Champions	2001*
AFC Champions	2003
Super Bowl XXXVIII Champions	2003*
AFC Champions	2004
Super Bowl XXXIX Champions	2004*

Super Bowls are played early the following year, but the game is counted as the championship of this season.

TOP: Bill Parcells, the 1994 NFL Coach of the Year.
RIGHT: Deion Branch rejoices after scoring a touchdown in Super Bowl XXXVIII.

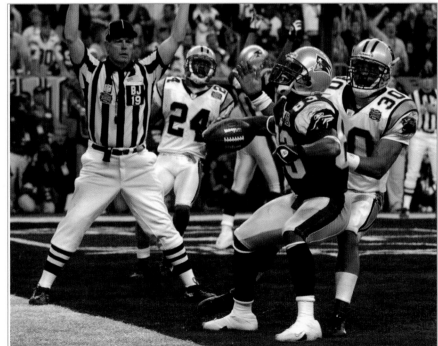

Pinpoints

T he history of a football team is made up of many smaller stories. These stories take place all over the map—not just in the city a team calls "home." Match the push-pins on these maps to the Team Facts and you will begin to see the story of the Patriots unfold!

TEAM FACTS

1 Boston, Massachusetts—*The team played here from 1960 to 1970.*

2 Foxborough, Massachusetts—*The team has played here since 1971.*

3 Nashville, Tennessee—*Bill Belichick was born here.*

4 Louise, Mississippi—*Houston Antwine was born here.*

5 San Mateo, California—*Tom Brady was born here.*

6 Aliquippa, Pennsylvania—*Ty Law was born here.*

7 San Antonio, Texas—*Steve Grogan was born here.*

8 Keewatin, Minnesota—*Gino Cappelletti was born here.*

9 Blythe, California—*Tony Eason was born here.*

10 Jacksonville, Florida—*The team won Super Bowl XXXIX here.*

11 Seattle, Washington—*Russ Francis was born here.*

12 Rapahidveg, Hungary—*Charlie Gogolak was born here.*

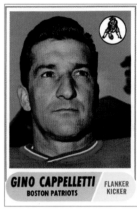

Gino Cappelletti

Play Ball

Football is a sport played by two teams on a field that is 100 yards long. The game is divided into four 15-minute quarters. Each team must have 11 players on the field at all times. The group that has the ball is called the offense. The group trying to keep the offense from moving the ball forward is called the defense.

A football game is made up of a series of "plays." Each play starts and ends with a referee's signal. A play begins when the center snaps the ball between his legs to the quarterback. The quarterback then gives the ball to a teammate, throws (or "passes") the ball to a teammate, or runs with the ball himself. The job of the defense is to tackle the player with the ball or stop the quarterback's pass. A play ends when the ball (or player holding the ball) is "down." The offense must move the ball forward at least 10 yards every four downs. If it fails to do so, the other team is given the ball. If the offense has not made 10 yards after three downs—and does not want to risk losing the ball—it can kick (or "punt") the ball to make the other team start from its own end of the field.

At each end of a football field is a goal line, which divides the field from the end zone. A team must run or pass the ball over the goal line to score a touchdown, which counts for six points. After scoring a touchdown, a team can try a short kick for one "extra point," or try again to run or pass across the goal line for two points. Teams can score three points from anywhere on the field by kicking the ball between the goal posts. This is called a field goal.

The defense can score two points if it tackles a player while he is in his own end zone. This is called a safety. The defense can also score points by taking the ball away from the offense and crossing the opposite goal line for a touchdown. The team with the most points after 60 minutes is the winner.

Football may seem like a very hard game to understand, but the more you play and watch football, the more "little things" you are likely to notice. The next time you are at a game, look for these plays:

 PLAY LIST

BLITZ—A play where the defense sends extra tacklers after the quarterback. If the quarterback sees a blitz coming, he passes the ball quickly. If he does not, he can end up on the bottom of a very big pile!

DRAW—A play where the offense pretends it will pass the ball, and then gives it to a running back. If the offense can "draw" the defense to the quarterback and his receivers, the running back should have lots of room to run.

FLY PATTERN—A play where a team's fastest receiver is told to "fly" past the defensive backs for a long pass. Many long touchdowns are scored on this play.

SQUIB KICK—A play where the ball is kicked a short distance on purpose. A squib kick is used when the team kicking off does not want the other team's fastest player to catch the ball and run with it.

SWEEP—A play where the ball-carrier follows a group of teammates moving sideways to "sweep" the defense out of the way. A good sweep gives the runner a chance to gain a lot of yards before he is tackled or forced out of bounds.

Glossary

FOOTBALL WORDS TO KNOW

AFL CHAMPIONSHIP—The game that decided the winner of the American Football League. This game was played from 1960 to 1969.

ALL-PRO—An honor given to the best players at their position at the end of each season.

AMERICAN FOOTBALL CONFERENCE (AFC)—One of two groups of teams that make up the National Football league. The winner of the AFC plays the winner of the National Football Conference (NFC) in the Super Bowl.

AMERICAN FOOTBALL LEAGUE (AFL)—The football league that began play in 1960, and later merged with the National Football League.

BACK-UP QUARTERBACK—A quarterback who only plays when the starter cannot.

BACKFIELD—The area behind the blockers, where the quarterback and running backs start each play.

COMPLETED—Threw a ball that was caught.

FIELD GOAL—A goal from the field, kicked over the crossbar and between the goal posts. A field goal is worth three points.

FUMBLED—Dropped the ball while carrying it.

INTERCEPTION—A pass caught by the defensive team.

MOST VALUABLE PLAYER (MVP)—The award given each year to the best player; also given to the best player in the Super Bowl.

NATIONAL FOOTBALL LEAGUE (NFL)—The league that started in 1920 and is still operating today.

PLAYOFFS—The games played after the regular season that determine who plays in the Super Bowl.

PRO BOWL—The NFL's all-star game, played after the Super Bowl.

PROFESSIONAL—A person or team that plays a sport for money. College players are not paid, so they are considered "amateurs."

RETURN MAN—A player whose job is to return punts and kickoffs.

ROOKIE—A player in his first year.

ROUT—Beat another team badly.

RUSHED—Ran with the football.

SUPER BOWL—The championship game of football, played between the winner of the American Football Conference (AFC) and National Football Conference (NFC).

UPRIGHTS—The two goal posts attached to the crossbar; field goals and extra points must be kicked between the uprights or they do not count.

OTHER WORDS TO KNOW

ACCOMPLISHED—Achieved or completed.

DECADES—Periods of 10 years.

DEDICATED—Devoted to a team or to a goal.

DOMINATE—To control through power.

HERITAGE—Historical background.

HUMBLE—Modest.

INVINCIBLE—Impossible to defeat.

MINUTEMAN—An American soldier from the Revolutionary War.

ON THE LINE—About to be won or lost.

PATRIOTIC—Showing love or loyalty to one's country.

PLAZAS—Open public spaces.

PRESS CONFERENCE—A meeting scheduled with writers and reporters.

STROKE—An injury to the brain caused by a lack of blood flow.

TAILBONE—The bone that protects the base of the spine.

TRADITION—A belief or custom that is handed down from generation to generation.

VETERAN—Someone who has experience doing a job.

Places to Go

ON THE ROAD

GILLETTE STADIUM
One Patriot Place
Foxborough, Massachusetts 02035
(508) 543-8200

THE PRO FOOTBALL HALL OF FAME
2121 George Halas Drive NW
Canton, Ohio 44708
(330) 456-8207

ON THE WEB

THE NATIONAL FOOTBALL LEAGUE   www.nfl.com
  • *Learn more about the National Football League*

THE NEW ENGLAND PATRIOTS   www.Patriots.com
  • *Learn more about the New England Patriots*

THE PRO FOOTBALL HALL OF FAME   www.profootballhof.com
  • *Learn more about football's greatest players*

ON THE BOOKSHELF

To learn more about the sport of football, look for these books at your library or bookstore:

  • Ingram, Scott. *A Football All-Pro*. Chicago, IL.: Heinemann Library, 2005.
  • Kennedy, Mike. *Football*. Danbury, CT.: Franklin Watts, 2003.
  • Suen, Anastasia. *The Story of Football*. New York, NY.: PowerKids Press, 2002.

Index

PAGE NUMBERS IN **BOLD** REFER TO ILLUSTRATIONS.

The Team

MARK STEWART has written more than 20 books on football, and over 100 sports books for kids. He grew up in New York City during the 1960s rooting for the Giants and Jets, and now takes his two daughters, Mariah and Rachel, to watch them play in their home state of New Jersey. Mark comes from a family of writers. His grandfather was Sunday Editor of *The New York Times* and his mother was Articles Editor of *The Ladies Home Journal* and *McCall's*. Mark has profiled hundreds of athletes over the last 20 years. He has also written several books about New York and New Jersey. Mark is a graduate of Duke University, with a degree in history. He lives with his daughters and wife, Sarah, overlooking Sandy Hook, NJ.

JASON AIKENS is the Collections Curator at the Pro Football Hall of Fame. He is responsible for the preservation of the Pro Football Hall of Fame's collection of artifacts and memorabilia and obtaining new donations of memorabilia from current players and NFL teams. Jason has a Bachelor of Arts in History from Michigan State University and a Masters in History from Western Michigan University where he concentrated on sports history. Jason has been working for the Pro Football Hall of Fame since 1997; before that he was an intern at the College Football Hall of Fame. Jason's family has roots in California

and has been following the St. Louis Rams since their days in Los Angeles, California. He lives with his wife Cynthia in Canton, OH.